The wonder of girls

"Innocence is the first flower of childhood"

"Make the **most** of **every** opportunity"

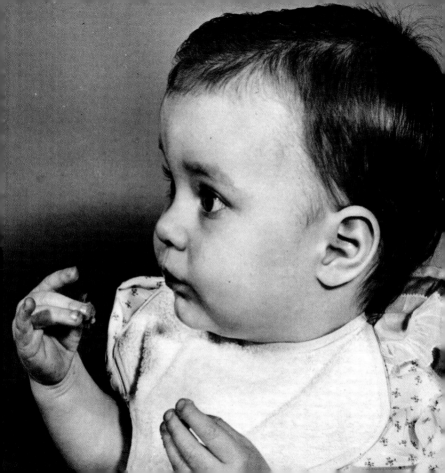

"What are
little girls
made of?
What are
little girls
made of?"

"Sugar and spice and all things nice
– that's what little girls are made of..."

– Nursery rhyme

"...or at least that's
the theory."

"Real
girls
are not afraid
of the dark..."

"...they like adventure..."

"...and they
don't
give up
when it all
goes wrong!"

"There are **times** when **every** girl needs a **hand**"

"Some girls are
gifted and clever..."

"but all girls can
take that step forward"

"The
knowingness
of little
girls..."

"...is
hidden in
their **curls**."

– Phillis McGinley

"Girls just want to have fun" – Cyndi Lauper